REVISED EDITION

RUBANK EDUCATIONAL LIBRARY No. 38

RUBANK Elementary METHOD

FLUTE or PICCOLO

A. C. PETERSEN

A FUNDAMENTAL COURSE FOR INDIVIDUAL OR LIKE-INSTRUMENT CLASS INSTRUCTION

RUBANK®

HAL•LEONARD® CORPORATION

7777 W. BLUEMOUND RD. P.O. BOX 13819 MILWAUKEE, WI 53213

LESSON 1

Whole Notes - Whole Rests

A. C. PETERSEN

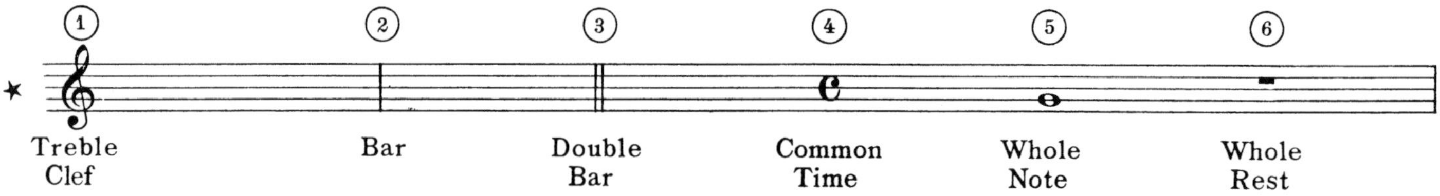

Attack each Note with the syllable "Tu" not "Thu"

✶ NOTE: Lessons 1 to 14

The first line of each lesson is a review of old problems and the introduction of new ones. Each one of these lines should be thoroughly gone through before proceeding with the lesson proper. The new problems should be clearly explained by the teacher, and the review problems clearly explained by the pupil. The pupil should be able to distinguish the review from the new.

Half Notes - Half Rests

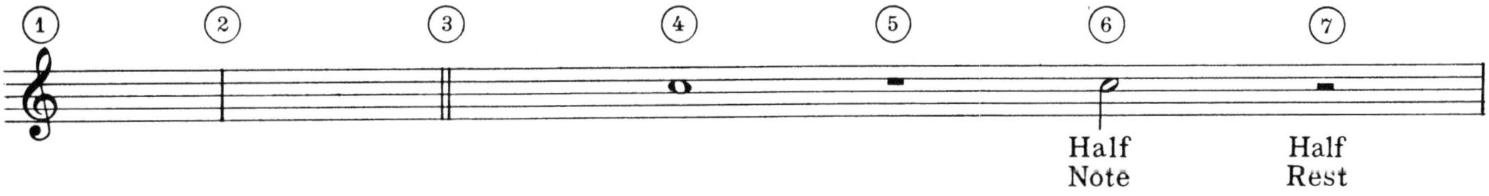

Melody

Counting Study

Quarter Notes-Quarter Rests

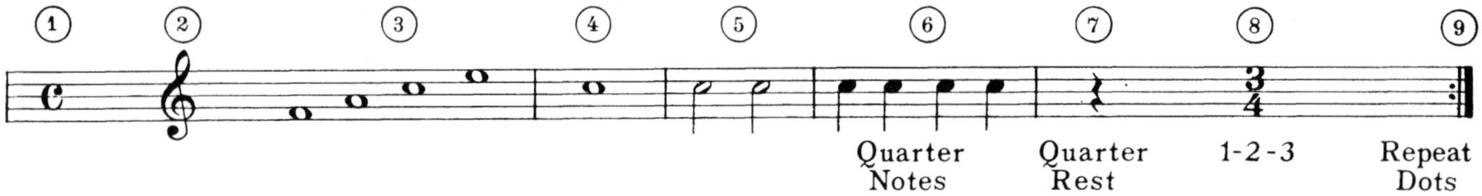

1 

2 

Melody

3 

4 

In Waltz Time

5 

Waltz Melody

6 

New Notes-Rhythmic Studies

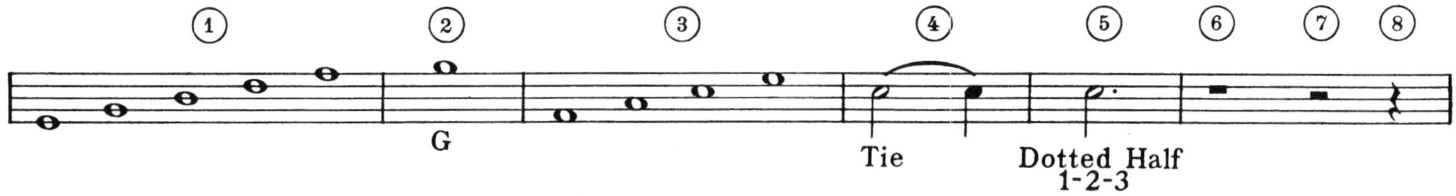

Dotted Half Notes

1
2
3

Interval Study

4

Extending the Range

5
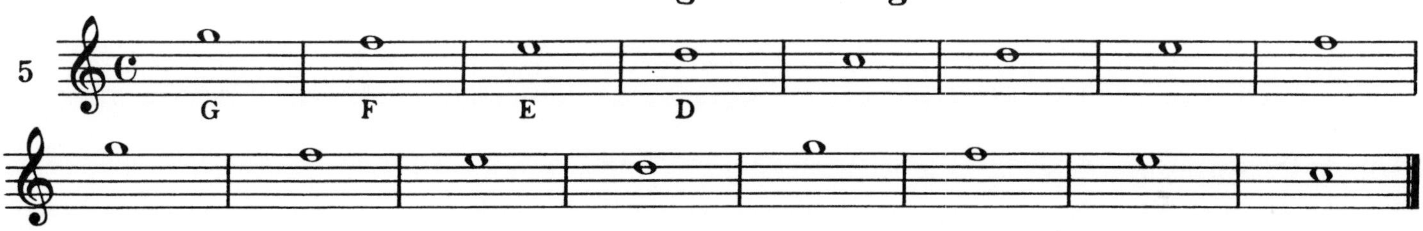

First Duet

6

Lightly Row

7

Study in Thirds

8

Development

1

2

3

Melody

4

Melody in $^3\!/_4$

5

Good Night, Ladies

College Song

6

High Note Study

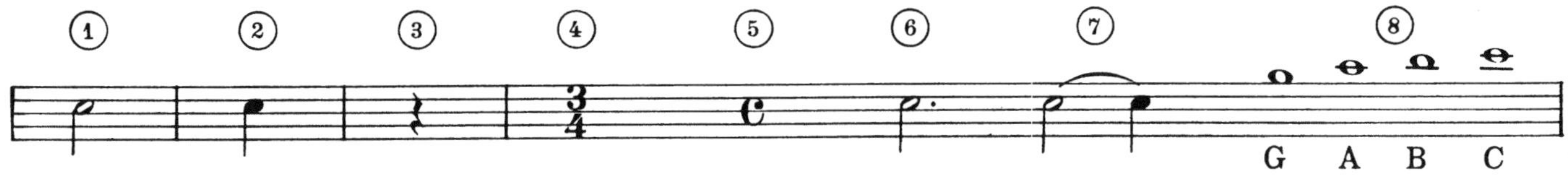

1 

C Major Chord

2 

C Major Chord

3 

C Major Scale

4 

C Major in Thirds

5 

6 

Chord Study

7 

F Major Studies

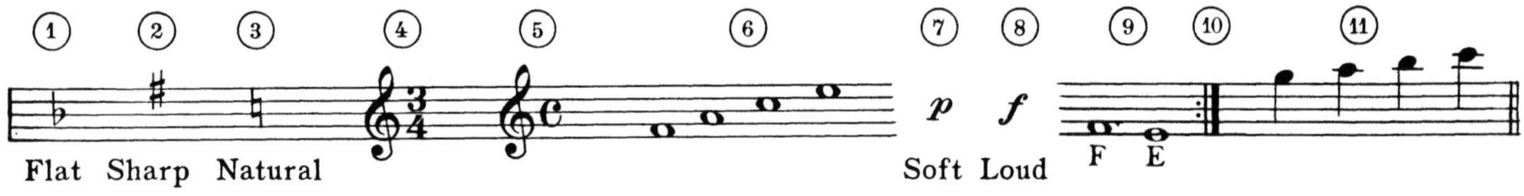

F Major Chord

F Major Scale

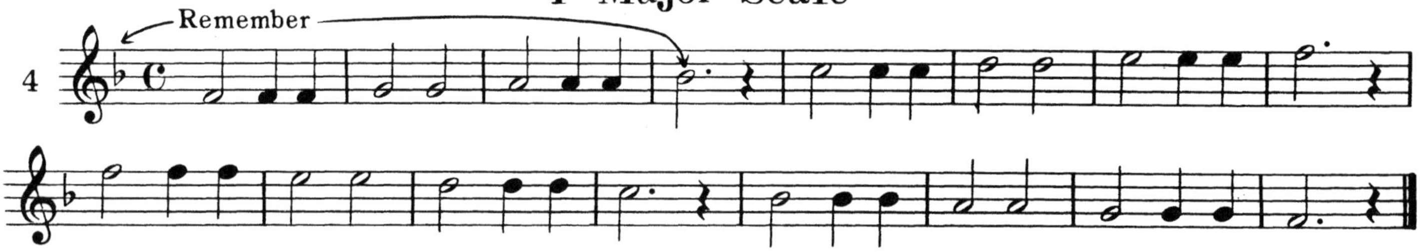

Melody in F Major

Duet in F Major

Eighth Note Studies

1

2

Long Long Ago-Key of C

3

Long Long Ago-Key of F

4

Folk Song

5

Technical Study

6

Dotted Quarter Notes

B♭ Major Chord

1

B♭ Major Scale

2

Dotted Quarter Notes

3
4
5

America in B♭

6

7

8

G Major Studies

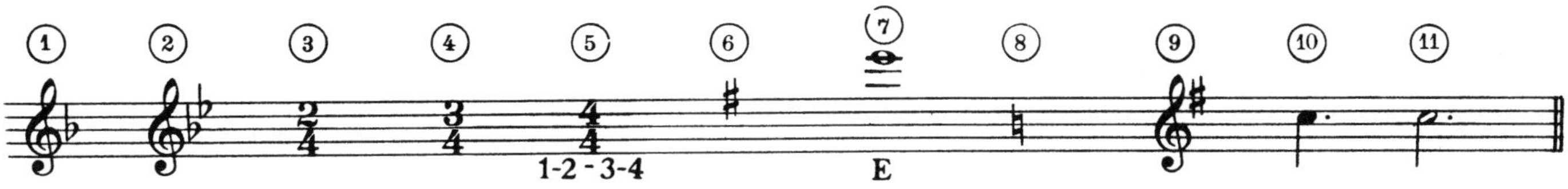

G Major Chord

1

G Major Scale

2

America in G

3

America in F

4

High Note Study

5

Development

Eighth Rest Studies

1
2
3

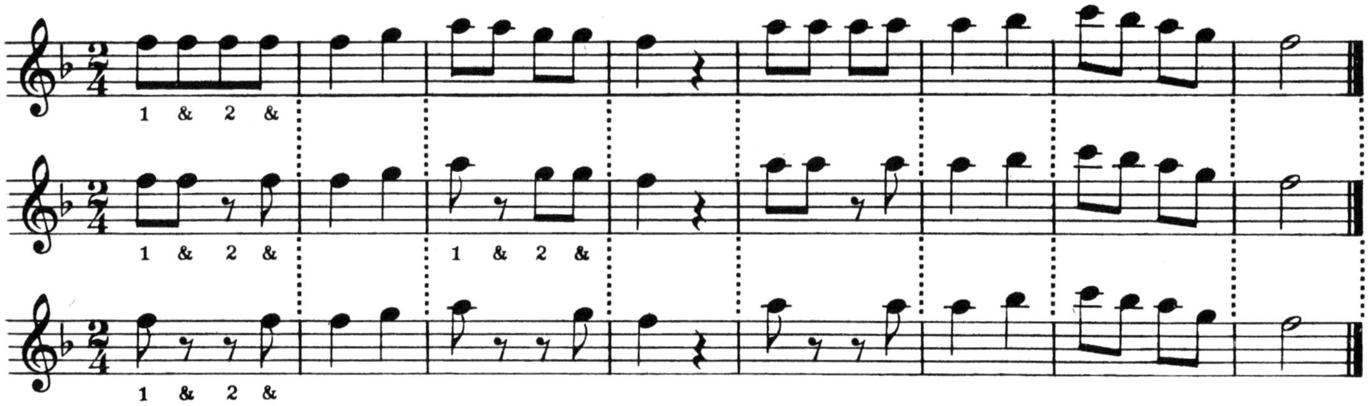

Technical Studies

4

5

Staccato Melody

6

Silent Night

FRANZ GRUBER

O Come, All Ye Faithful

J. REALING

The First Noel

French, 18th Century

D Major Studies

Melody in D Major

Chord Studies

Blue Bells of Scotland

Scotch Folk Song

Andante moderato

Slurs

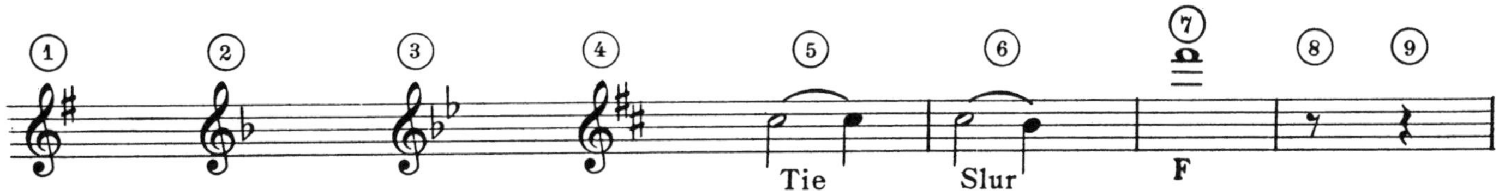

Slow Slurs

Slur both groups of two, and groups of four notes.

1

Fast Slurs

2

Folk Melody

Slur both ways

3

F Major Scale

4

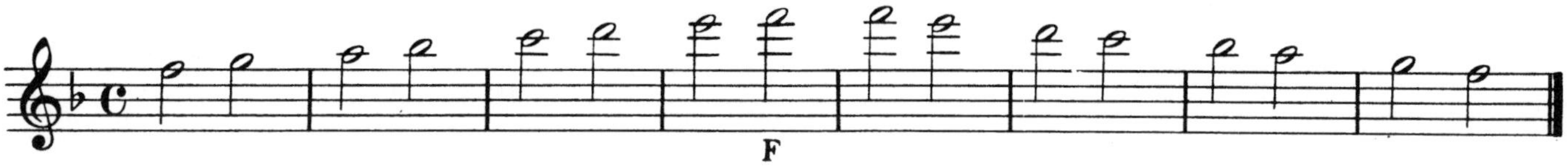

Rhythmic Studies

1

2

3

D Major Chord Study

4

Counting Studies

1

2

3

Duo Plaisir

4

Alla Breve

Ties

Melody

Minor Scale Studies

C Major

1 

A Minor Melodic

2 

A Minor Harmonic

3 

Triads

4 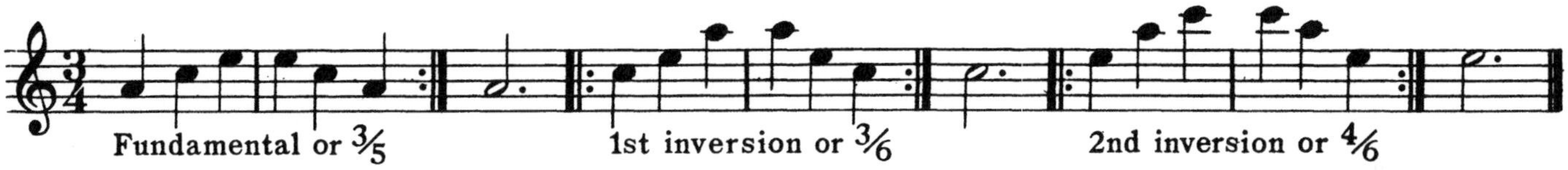

5 

6 

7 

8 

Melody in A Minor

Andante

9 

6/8 Rhythms

1

2

3

Melody

4

5

F Major Scale

6

E♭ Major Studies

E♭ Major Chord

1 

E♭ Major Scale

2 

3 

4 

E♭ Major Chord

5 

Melody in E♭ Major

Allegretto

6 

Rhythmic Studies

1

2

Melody with Accidentals

3

Sixteenth Notes

1 2 3

4

Melody

5

Technical Study

6

Sixteenth Note Studies

1

Chord Study

2

Study for Articulation

3

Fast Fingering Melody

4

ANK
FLUTE AND PICCOLO CHART
G Sharp Key
PETERSEN

E	F	G	A	B	C	D	E	F	G	A	B	C
1	1	1	1	1	1		1	1	1		1	1
x	x	x	x	x		x	x	x		x	x	
2	2	2	2			2	2		2	2		2
3	3	3				3		3	3		3	3
												x
4	4						4	4		4		4
5							5					
											6x	
x	x	x	x	x	x	x	x	x	x	x	x (Opt.)*	

*Optional

♯ ♭	♯ ♭	♯	♭	♯ ♭	♯ ♭	♯ ♭	♯ ♭	♯ ♭
1	1	1	1		1	1		
x	x	x	x♭		x	x		x
2	2				2		2	
3	3				3	3	3	
	x				x		x	
		4			4			4
					5			5x
6 or 5*					6	6 or 5*		
x	x	x	x	x	x	x	x	x

used in rapid passages to facilitate fingering.

RU
BOEHM SYSTE
With Clos
By A. C

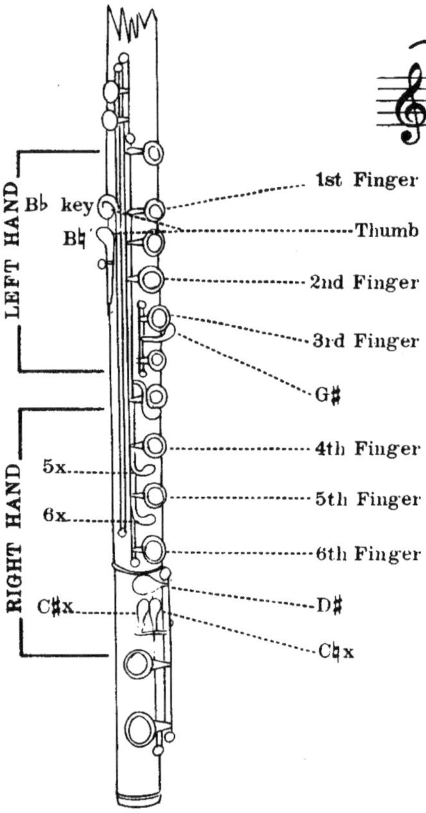

Flute only

	C	D	E	F	G	A	B	C
1st Finger	1	1	1	1	1	1	1	1
Thumb	X	X	X	X	X	X	X	
2nd Finger	2	2	2	2	2	2		
3rd Finger	3	3	3	3	3			
G♯								
4th Finger	4	4	4	4				
5th Finger	5	5	5					
6th Finger	6	6						
D♯			X	X	X	X	X	X
	C♮x							

Thumb on B♮ key

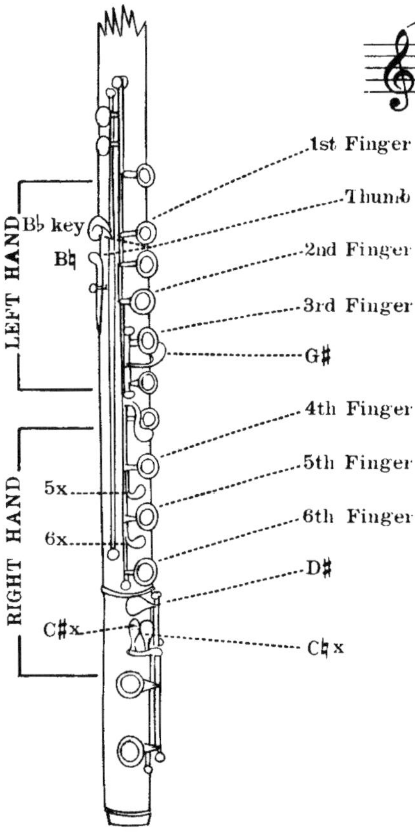

Flute only

	C♯ D♭	D♯ E♭	F♯ G♭	G♯ A♭	A♯	B♭	C♯ D♭	D♯
1st Finger	1	1	1	1	1	1		
Thumb	X	X	X	X	X	X♭		X
2nd Finger	2	2	2	2				2
3rd Finger	3	3	3	3				3
G♯				X				
4th Finger	4	4			4			4
5th Finger	5	5						5
6th Finger	6	6	6 or 5*					6
D♯		X	X	X	X	X	X	X
	C♯x							

Thumb on B♮ key

*The 6th finger is preferred; the 5th finger m

Dotted Eighth Notes

1

2

3

4

The Christmas Tree

5

Melody

6

Joy to the World

G. F. HANDEL

7

Triplet Studies

Trill Study

Syncopation

Melody

Development of Reading

1

Ballet Scene

Duet

Waltz tempo

2

D Minor Studies

Etude in D Minor

A Major and F♯ Minor Studies

A Major

1 

F♯ Minor Melodic

2 

F♯ Minor Harmonic

3 

A Major Chord Study

4 

Play with both three beats and one beat to the measure.

5 

Melody

6 

Articulations

Triplet Articulation

1

Articulation Study

2

Rhythmic Chord Studies

Rhythmic Development

Chromatic Scale Studies

Keep thumb on natural key

1

2

3

Octave Study

4

5

Rhythm Studies

1 

Melody

2 

Etude for Counting

3 

A♭ Major Studies

A♭ Major

1

2

A♭ Major Etude

3

Trill Studies

4

5

Variety Rhythm Studies

1

2

Syncopation

3

Petite Duet

E Major Studies

E Major Scale

1

2

Chord Study

3

Melody

Andante

4

Waltz Study

1

Scale Study

2
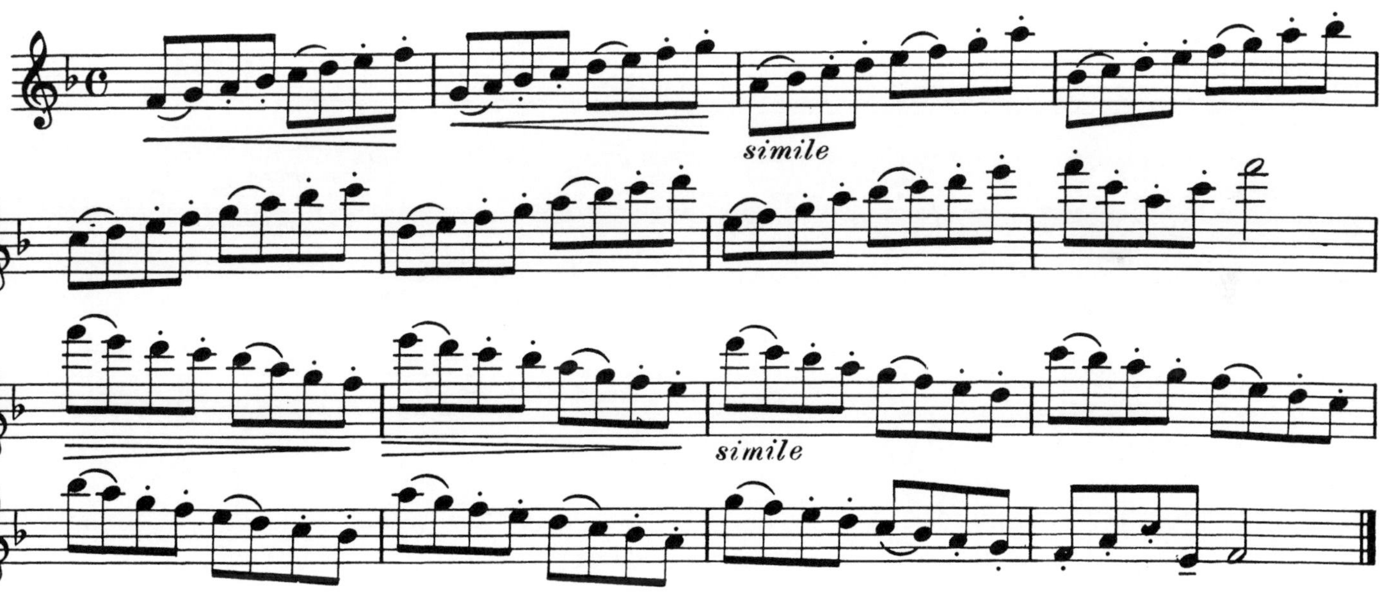

Octave Study

3

Etude

1

2

Examination Lesson I

1 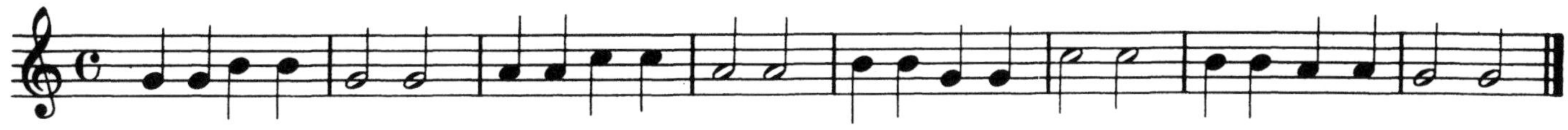

2 

3 

4 

5 

6 

7 

8 

9 

10 

11 

12 

Examination Lesson II

Believe Me, If All Those Endearing Young Charms

MOORE

Rock of Ages

THOMAS HASTINGS

Minuet from Orpheus

GLUCK

Gavotte

GOSSEC

America the Beautiful

SAMUEL A. WARD

Old Folks at Home
(Swanee River)

STEPHEN C. FOSTER

Come Back to Erin

BARNARD

Scarf Dance

CHAMINADE

Welsh Folk Song

Lullaby

Andante con moto

BRAHMS